First World War
and Army of Occupation
War Diary
France, Belgium and Germany

33 DIVISION
Divisional Troops
166 Brigade Royal Field Artillery
1 October 1915 - 31 January 1917

WO95/2413/5

The Naval & Military Press Ltd
www.nmarchive.com
Published in association with The National Archives

Published by

The Naval & Military Press Ltd

Unit 10 Ridgewood Industrial Park,

Uckfield, East Sussex,

TN22 5QE England

Tel: +44 (0) 1825 749494

www.naval-military-press.com

www.nmarchive.com

This diary has been reprinted in facsimile from the original. Any imperfections are inevitably reproduced and the quality may fall short of modern type and cartographic standards.

© Crown Copyright
Images reproduced by permission of The National Archives, London, England, 2015.

Contents

Document type	Place/Title	Date From	Date To
Heading	WO95/2413/5		
Heading	33rd Division Divl Artillery 166th Brigade R.F.A. Oct 1915-Feb 1917		
Heading	33rd 166th Bde. R.F.A. Vol 1 October & December 1915		
Heading	From O.C. 166 Brigade R.F.A. To D.A.G 3rd Echelon		
War Diary	No. 7 Camp, Sling, Bulford	01/10/1915	03/11/1915
War Diary	No. 7 Camp. Sling, Bulford, Salisbury, Wilts	03/11/1915	29/12/1915
War Diary	Guarbecque Pas-De-Calais	01/01/1916	27/02/1916
War Diary	Annequin	10/03/1916	31/03/1916
War Diary		02/04/1916	28/05/1916
Heading	War Diary D 166 R.F.A Late D/167 R.F.A. Original Copy Period 1.5.16 To 31.5.16 Vol 1		
War Diary	Annequin	01/05/1916	10/06/1916
War Diary	Gorre	17/06/1916	25/06/1916
War Diary	Annequin	06/06/1916	30/06/1916
Heading	War Diary Headquarters, 166th Brigade R.F.A. (33rd Division) July 1916		
War Diary	Annequin	06/07/1916	07/07/1916
War Diary	Bethune	08/07/1916	29/07/1916
Heading	33rd Divisional Artillery 166th Brigade Royal Field Artillery August 1916		
War Diary		02/08/1916	30/08/1916
Operation(al) Order(s)	14th Divisional Artillery Operation Order No.58 By Brigadier General W. Sandys. C.M.G.	23/08/1916	23/08/1916
Miscellaneous	Time Table To Accompany 14th Div'l Artillery Operation Order No. 38	24/08/1916	24/08/1916
Map	Map No. X18		
Miscellaneous	Supported 33rd Division in Operations Orderd in O.O. 38 (attachee)		
War Diary	Mametz (Somme)	01/09/1916	12/09/1916
War Diary	Arras	13/09/1916	31/10/1916
Miscellaneous	156th Brigade R.F.A. For Information	11/11/1916	11/11/1916
Miscellaneous	Table "A"		
Map	Map Shewing German Trenches		
War Diary		01/11/1916	23/11/1916
War Diary	Airaines	01/12/1916	31/12/1916
War Diary	Field	12/12/1916	28/12/1916
Miscellaneous	Received From Headquarters 33rd Division the undermentioned War Diary for Jan 1917		
Miscellaneous	D.A.G., G.H.Q. 3rd Echelon	09/02/1917	09/02/1917
War Diary		01/01/1917	31/01/1917
Miscellaneous	92 Infantry Brigade	16/11/1916	16/11/1916
Operation(al) Order(s)	166th Brigade R.F.A. Order No 4		
Miscellaneous	Appendix No 1		

W995/2413 (5)

W995/2413 (5)

33RD DIVISION
DIVL ARTILLERY

166TH BRIGADE R.F.A.
OCT ~~DEC~~ 1915 - FEB 1917

BROKEN UP

166th Bde: R.F.A.
Vol I.

33rd

October & December
1915

Jan 1916

From O.C. 166 Brigade R.F.A
To D.A.G. 3rd Echelon.

Herewith war Diary period
October 1st to Jan 31st. 1916

Simmons
Lt.
for Col. 166 R.F.A

10.2.16

Army Form C. 2118.

WAR DIARY
or
INTELLIGENCE SUMMARY.
(Erase heading not required.)

October 1915.

Instructions regarding War Diaries and Intelligence Summaries are contained in F.S. Regs., Part II. and the Staff Manual respectively. Title pages will be prepared in manuscript.

Place: No.7 Camp, Sling, Bulford.

Date	Hour	Summary of Events and Information	Remarks and references to Appendices
1st.		Officers were posted as follows:-	
		Colonel A.Goff C.M.G.	
		Adjutant Lieut E.G.Lutyens.	
		Orderly Officer 2nd Lt. S.M.Wood.	
		Captain E.T.P.Goodyear, "A" Battery.	
		Lieut. W.L.Powrie, "	
		2nd Lieut. P.J.McDonald, "	
		" K.A.Hayward, "	
		Captain T.E.Durie, "B"	
		2nd Lieut. A.O.I.Brownlee, "	
		" V.Lewis, "	
		" F.W.Elliott, "	
		Captain W.F.Tuthill, "C"	
		2nd Lieut. H.Freeman, "	
		" C.W.Weekes, "	
		" C.S.Peerless, "	
		Captain G.Fetherston, "D"	
		2nd Lieut. C.R.Wadman, "	
		" C.Challen, "	
		" A.H.Cane, "	
		Lieut. R.S.Limpenny, Ammn: Col:	
		2nd Lieut. E.T.Winbush, "	
		" F.Colvill, "	
11th		9 Horses received.	
16th		Lieut.J.O.Baker. R.A.M.C. was attached for duty with the Brigade.	
17th		15 Horses joined.	

Shorro [signature] for Col.
COMMANDING 156TH BRIGADE. R.F.A.

Army Form C. 2118.

WAR DIARY
or
INTELLIGENCE SUMMARY.
(Erase heading not required.)

OCTOBER 1915. (Contd).

Instructions regarding War Diaries and Intelligence Summaries are contained in F.S. Regs. Part II. and the Staff Manual respectively. Title pages will be prepared in manuscript.

Place	Date	Hour	Summary of Events and Information	Remarks and references to Appendices
No.7. Camp, Sling, Bulford.	20th		The Batteries moved and billeted, "A" & "B" at CHARLTON, "C" & "D" RUSHALL, returning to SLING on the 22nd.	
	26th		Lieut. W.L. Powrie transferred to 33rd D.A.C.	
	23rd		8 G.S. Wagons received.	
	26th		2nd Lieut J.R.B. Turner joined.	
	26th		Capt. W.F. Tuthill transferred to 39th Division.	
	27th		2nd Lieut. P.J. McDonald transferred to 1a Reserve Bde, Newcastle	
	27th		2nd Lieut. E.C. Ormond joined.	
	29th		2nd Lieut. K.J. Snowden joined.	
	30th		2nd Lieut. G. Coleman joined.	

Simmons
Commanding 186th Brigade R.F.A.

Army Form C. 2118.

WAR DIARY
or
INTELLIGENCE SUMMARY.

(Erase heading not required.)

NOVEMBER 1915.

Instructions regarding War Diaries and Intelligence Summaries are contained in F.S. Regs., Part II. and the Staff Manual respectively. Title pages will be prepared in manuscript.

Place	Date	Hour	Summary of Events and Information	Remarks and references to Appendices
Bulford.	1st		2/Lieut G.R.G.Collins joined.	
	1st		2/Lieut A.R.Tucker joined.	
	1st		2/Lieut J.H.K.Rayson joined.	
	2nd		Capt.D.Spurling transferred from 33rd D.A.C.	
No.7 Camp, Sling,	2nd		Lieut R.S.Limpenny transferred to 33rd D.A.C.	
	3rd		The strength of Officers for the Brigade was completed as follows:-	

Colonel A.Goff C.M.G.,
Lieut. E.G.Lutyens, (Adjutant)
2/Lieut.S.M.Wood, (Orderly Officer)
Lieut.Nicholson A.V.C. (Vet: Officer attached)
Lieut.J.O.Baker R.A.M.C.

"A" Battery.
Capt.E.T.P.Goodyear
2/Lieut.K.A.Hayward
2/Lieut.K.J.Snowden
2/Lieut.E.C.Ormond

"B" Battery.
Capt.T.E.Durie
2/Lieut.A.O.I.Brownlee
2/Lieut.F.W.Elliott
2/Lieut.G.R.G.Collins

"C" Battery.
2/Lieut.H.Freeman
2/Lieut.C.R.Wadman
2/Lieut.C.W.Weekes
2/Lieut.C.S.Peerless

"D" Battery.
Capt.G.Fetherstone
2/Lieut.G.Coleman
2/Lieut.J.R.B.Turner
2/Lieut.A.R.Tucker

Ammunition Col:
Capt.D.Spurling,
2/Lieut.F.Colvill,
2/Lieut.C.Challen,
2/Lieut.J.H.K.Rayson,

Army Form C. 2118.

WAR DIARY
or
INTELLIGENCE SUMMARY.
(Erase heading not required.)

NOVEMBER 1915. (Contd).

Place	Date	Hour	Summary of Events and Information	Remarks and references to Appendices
No.7 Camp, Sling, Bulford, Salisbury, Wilts.	3rd (Contd)		Officers i/c details. 2/Lieut.V.Lewis. 2/Lieut.E.T.Winbush.	
	4th		4 horses joined.	
	5th		3 horses transferred.	
	7th		2/Lieut.E.T.Winbush transferred to Brigade Ammunition Column, and 2/Lieut.C.Challen detailed as an Officer i/c details.	
	10th 14th 16th		Firing practice at Larkhill.	
	15th		Lieut.D.Manners-Davis joined as Officer i/c details, vice 2/Lt.V.Lewis	
	16th		2/Lieut.L.H.Blomenstok joined and was posted to "B" Battery.	
	"		2/Lieut.K.A.Hayward transferred from "A" Battery to "B". 2/Lieut. G.R.G.Collins transferred from "B" Battery to "D".	
	18th		12 Wagons, 24 Horses, and 12 Drivers arrived from A.S.C.Divisional Train.(East Anglian).	
	20th		Lieut.A.O.L.Brownlee transferred to 6c Reserve Brigade, Newcastle.	
	25th		2/Lieut.H.Freeman promoted to Captain.	

Simmons Col. R.F.A.
COMMANDING 100TH BRIGADE R.F.A.

WAR DIARY
or
INTELLIGENCE SUMMARY.

Army Form C. 2118.

Place: December 1915

Date	Hour	Summary of Events and Information	Remarks and references to Appendices
9th		Lt. D.M. Coffin took command of "A" Battery vice Capt. E.T.P. Goodyear to Hospital	
12th		The Brigade left SLING CAMP and entrained at AMESBURY Stn.	
12th		The Brigade embarked at SOUTHAMPTON.	
13th		The Brigade dis-embarked at LE HAVRE.	
14th		The Brigade de-trained at THIENNES.	
15th		The Brigade billeted in the village of GUARBECQUE.	
20th		East Anglian Divisional Train returned to their own unit	
22nd		Lt. D.M. Coffin promoted to Captain.	
23rd		2nd Lt. F. D'A. Cooper joined and was posted to "B" Battery	
"		2nd Lt. R.A. Swinton joined and was posted to "D" Battery.	
29		2Lt. K.J. Snowdon attended the 2nd Course 1st Army Artillery School at LETTRES.	

SMMoody
Major
Commanding 1st/1st E. Anglian Brigade R.F.A.

WAR DIARY or INTELLIGENCE SUMMARY.

Army Form C. 2118.

January 1916.

Place	Date	Hour	Summary of Events and Information	Remarks and references to Appendices
GUARBECQUE	1st		2nd Lt. J.R.B. TURNER. Transfers from "D" Battery to the Ammunition Column. 2nd Lt. J.K. RAYSON transfers from Ammunition Column to "D" Battery.	
	4th		CAPT. H. FREEMAN attended 4th Artillery Course at AIRE. M. C.L. BATTIAUX reports for duty with the Brigade as Interpreter.	
	10th		2nd Lt. E.T. WINBUSH transfers from 166th B.A.C. to 33rd D.A.C. 2nd Lt. H.H. HEWITT. transfers from 33rd D.A.C. to 166th B.A.C.	
			Brigade Baths completes fitted at GUARBECQUE.	
	20th		"C" Battery under Capt. H. FREEMAN were inspected by Gen. JOFFRE near LILLERS.	
	23rd		2nd Lt. R.A. SWINTON admitted to hospital.	
	25th		2nd Lt. C.J. LUTYENS joins and was posted to D Battery.	
	30th		Divisional Manoeuvres. The Brigade billeted at SERNY.	
	31st		The Brigade returned to GUARBECQUE.	

Army Form C. 2118.

January 1916 (cont.)

WAR DIARY
or
INTELLIGENCE SUMMARY.
(Erase heading not required.)

Instructions regarding War Diaries and Intelligence Summaries are contained in F.S. Regs., Part II and the Staff Manual respectively. Title pages will be prepared in manuscript.

Place	Date	Hour	Summary of Events and Information	Remarks and references to Appendices
GUARBECQUE PAS-DE-CALAIS			During the month all officers & a proportion of the personnel of the units were attached to the 2nd Division RA for instruction. During the latter part of the month "B" Battery took over to the horses 48th Battery RFA and half "D" Battery took over from 46th Battery RFA during 7 days.	

February 1916

WAR DIARY
or
INTELLIGENCE SUMMARY.

166 Brigade. R.F.A., Army Form C. 2118.
February 1916

(Erase heading not required.)

Place	Date	Hour	Summary of Events and Information	Remarks and references to Appendices
	2nd		2Lt. C. J. LUTYENS transferred from "D" Battery to "Ammunition Column"	
			2Lt. H. H. HEWITT transferred from "Ammunition Column" to "C" Battery.	
	15th		2Lt. A. DRAKE - BROCKMAN joined from posts temporarily to "D" Battery	
	13th		"A" Battery 166 tooR over from A/63 in the "Z" sector at Cambrin	
	24th		Rest of 166 Bde took over from 63rd Bde, who moved to Vermelles	
	25th		Col. Goss took over the command of "Z" Group from Col. Short	
	26th		Front covered by "Z" Group, front line trench A.21.d.9½ to A.28.d.1½ (ref 36c NW1 1:10,000)	
			We were behind the 19th 98th 100th Infantry Brigades; with "D" Group	
			on our right to the South and "A" Group on our left	
	27th		Orders of 27th.... Adopt "THAW Precautions"	

MARCH 1916.

Army Form C. 2118.

166 RFA Vol 3

XXXIII

WAR DIARY or INTELLIGENCE SUMMARY.

Place: ANNEQUIN

Date	Hour	Summary of Events and Information	Remarks and references to Appendices
10th		2/Lt. C.J.Lutyens admitted to Hospital sick.	
13th		2/Lt. Drake-Brockman A, Proceeded to LARKHILL for Arty.Course.	
17th		2/Lt. C.J.Lutyens evacuated to England per H.S. S.S.Brighton.	
,,		2/Lt. F.J.Hacquoil joined and posted to "A" Battery.	
18th	5.30pm to 7.30pm	Gave assistance to "D" Group Artillery,12th Division.	
26th		2/Lt. F.J.Hacquoil transferred to Brigade Ammunition Column.	
28th		2/Lt. K.A.Hayward wounded. AUCHY Section Lt-Col.Harris took over command of Auchy Group Artillery, now made up as under:- (AUCHY Section being new name for Z Group.) A/166, B/166, C/166, D/162, ½ D/156, D/167 (Hows), ½ C/167 (Hows); 166 B.A.C. supplying ammunition to "Z" Group.	
,,		166 Brigade H.Q. moved to BETHUNE.	
,,		Col.A.H.S.Goff C.M.G., took over temporary command of 33rd Divisional Artillery.	
30th.		Leave opened.	
,,		2/Lt.F.W.J.Colson and 2/Lt.D.M.Fell attached to Brigade. Authority:- XIth Corps No. A 19/321 dated 26/3/16	
31st		2/Lt.K.A.Hayward evacuated to England per H.S. S.S.Dieppe.	

Vol 4
XXXII
166 RFA

Army Form C. 2118.

WAR DIARY
or
INTELLIGENCE SUMMARY.
(Erase heading not required.)

APRIL 1916.

Instructions regarding War Diaries and Intelligence Summaries are contained in F.S. Regs., Part II. and the Staff Manual respectively. Title pages will be prepared in manuscript.

Place	Date	Hour	Summary of Events and Information	Remarks and references to Appendices
	2nd		2 Officers and 20 men from 39th Division per Battery attached for instruction.	
	"		Colonel Rudkin, 39th Divisional Artillery, attached to 166th Brigade H.Q. for 2 days.	
	8th		Orders issued regarding wearing of steel helmets to and from the trenches. Traffic Control orders revised.	
	12th		2/Lt. F.J. Hacquoil transferred to 33rd D.A.C.,	
	11th		2/Lt. G.F. Gush transferred from 33rd D.A.C. and posted to B.A.C.	
	14th		2/Lt. H.H. Hewitt transferred from C/166 to A/166.	
	"		2/Lt. J.R.B. Turner transferred from B.A.C. to D/166.	
	15th		2/Lt. O.B. Gallie posted to B.A.C.	
	20th		2/Lt. R.A. Swinton posted to B.A.C.	
	25th		Col. A.H.S. Goff proceeded on leave to England. Capt. T.E. Durie temporarily in command.	
	29th		Battery wagon lines moved their positions on account of hostile shelling.	

COMMANDING 166TH BRIGADE, R.F.A.

WAR DIARY or INTELLIGENCE SUMMARY

Army Form C. 2118.

MAY 1916.

Place	Date	Hour	Summary of Events and Information	Remarks and references to Appendices
	11th.		2/Lieut. F.W.J.Colson C/166 transferred to 33rd D.A.C.	
	13th		Colonel A.H.S.Goff C.M.G., returned from leave.	
	13/14th (night of)		C/166 withdrew from the line and proceeded to First Army Training Area for manoeuvres.	
	14th/15th		Position taken over by A/162.	
	16th		Col.A.H.S.Goff relieved Lt.Col.Harris (162 Bde.H.Q) and took command of AUCHY Group.	
	"		166 B.A.C. (Capt.D.Spurling, 2/Lt.G.F.Gush, 2/Lt.O.B.Gallie) becomes 3rd Section D.A.C. D/166 (Capt.G.Fetherston, 2/Lt.G.Coleman, 2/Lt.A.R.Tucker, 2/Lt.J.R.B.Turner, 2/Lt.J.H.K.Rayson) becomes C/167. D/167 (Howitzer Battery), (Capt.W.A.T.Barstow, 2/Lt.F.G.M. Gardner, 2/Lt.L.W.Porterfield, 2/Lt.K.W.Milnes, and 2/Lt.J.C.KERR) becomes D/166 (How: Battery)	
	21st.		2/Lt.F.Colvill, 166 B.A.C. posted to C/166.	
	22nd.		C/166 Returned from manoeuvres. Took over A/167 in the line.	
	25th.		2/Lt.S.W.Swaine posted to the Brigade, and attached to B/166.	
	27th.		" " " transferred to A/166.	
	26th		Lt.Col. Harris (166 Bde.H.Q.) relieved Col.A.H.S.Goff and took over command of AUCHY Group. 166 Bde.H.Q. returned to BETHUNE.	
	28th		Lieut.E.G.Lutyens (Adjutant 166 Bde) took over temporary command of A/156.	
	"		2/Lieut.S.M.Wood (Orderly Officer) took over duties of Adjutant.	
	"		2/Lieut.E.C.Ormond, A/166, took over duties of Orderly Officer.	

D/166 RFA Vol 1 33

WAR DIARY.
D. 166 R F A
late D/167 R.F.A.
Original Copy.
Period 1.5.16 to
31. 5. 16.

Army Form C. 2118

D Bty 166 Bde R.F.A.

WAR DIARY
or
INTELLIGENCE SUMMARY
(Erase heading not required.)

Place	Date	Hour	Summary of Events and Information	Remarks and references to Appendices
ANNEQUIN	1.5.16		An extern covering AUCHY SECTION. A quiet day, hostile artillery inactive	WAD
	2.5.16	6.30am	Enemy was active with Minenwerfer. A small mine was exploded by Germans near MAD POINT.	WAD
	3.5.16		The battery retaliated at request of Right Inf. Coln. Commander. A M.G. Emplacement was engaged.	WAD
	4.5.16		3 M.G. Emplacements were engaged. The parapet & wire were damaged. The enemy artillery was more active.	WAD
	5.5.16		Registration of Enemy's front line between MIDNIGHT and GIBSON craters. Parapet damaged. Neighbourhood of ANNEQUIN was shelled by 15cm Howitzers.	WAD
	6.5.16	6am	A mine was exploded by Germans just S. of TWIN CRATERS. Our infantry occupied the crater immediately. Hostile Minenwerfer were active. The position of the Minenwerfer was observed & registered.	WAD
		6 pm	The Enemy started a bombardment with artillery & Minenwerfer. The latter was engaged & silenced.	WAD

Army Form C. 2118

WAR DIARY
or
INTELLIGENCE SUMMARY
(Erase heading not required.)

Instructions regarding War Diaries and Intelligence Summaries are contained in F. S. Regs., Part II. and the Staff Manual respectively. Title Pages will be prepared in manuscript.

Place	Date	Hour	Summary of Events and Information	Remarks and references to Appendices
ANNEQUIN	7/5/16		A quiet day.	WD/21
"	8/5/16	4.30am	Abnormal railway activity was observed lasting until 10 am in neighbourhood of DOUVRIN. Afternoon a quiet day	WD/21
"	9/5/16		A quiet day on our front. No hostile shelling.	WD/21
"	10/5/16		Hostile minenwerfer active and fired on	WD/21
"	11/5/16		Fired 133 rounds at HOHENZOLLERN REDOUBT in support of 15th Division. ANNEQUIN was shelled in afternoon by 10 x 15 cm. fairly heavily.	WD/21
"	12/5/16	6.30 p.m	ANNEQUIN shelled by 7.7 x 15 cm.	WD/21
"	13/5/16		A quiet day with very little hostile shelling. Fired at revolver gun 18 rounds and apparently destroyed it.	WD/21
"	14/5/16		ANNEQUIN shelled by 10 cm. in afternoon. Enemy's working party dispersed	WD/21
"	15/5/16		Enemy exploded small mine between BOYAU 19 & 20 and followed it up by bombardment of front line trenches	WD/21
		7 pm to 8 pm.	Enemy shelled ANNEQUIN with 10 cm x 15 cm. Fired 100 rounds in support of raid by our infantry at 10 p.m. A premature occurred with No 6 gun, killing Gnr Edwards & severely wounding Cpl. Boyer.	WD/21
"	16/5/16		Fairly quiet day.	WD/21
"	17/5/16		Registered Hindenburg, Foss & Corons Trench. Enemy shelled ANNEQUIN fairly heavily with 10 x 15 cm. A good number of retrogmatory shells were dropped close to the battery.	WD/21

Army Form C. 2118

WAR DIARY
or
INTELLIGENCE SUMMARY
(Erase heading not required.)

Instructions regarding War Diaries and Intelligence Summaries are contained in F. S. Regs., Part II. and the Staff Manual respectively. Title Pages will be prepared in manuscript.

Place	Date	Hour	Summary of Events and Information	Remarks and references to Appendices
ANNEQUIN	18/5/16	3 a.m.	80 rounds fired at enemy's trenches at A.2.f.a	
"	19/5/16	1.30pm	Machine gun emplacement fired at, direct hit which destroyed it, also front line damaged & wire cut.	WARR
"	22/5/16	7.45 AM	Fired in retaliation for big Minnie	WARR
"	23/5/16	6.15 PM	Registered shot corrected battery received with N.C.T. & CORDITE cartridges	WARR
"	24/5/16	2 PM	Fired on Bosch keep in retaliation for big MINNIE which were silenced	WARR
"	25/5/16	6.15 PM	28 rds on M/G emplacement A.25.c.57, unit in front line also damaged. A terrative started in WSgun, wounding gunt. water & junt. Page't.	WARR
"	27/5/16	2.30 AM	20 rds on trenches around MINE POINT.	WARR
"	"	12.30 PM	" MINE SHAFT A.28.a 15.80. Effect good, trenches damaged, M/S entrance destroyed, + one shot entered dug-out & destroying it.	WARR
"	28.5.16	4 PM	Trench junction A.28.a.4.1. + A.28.a.7.3 registered	WARR
"	29.5.16	11.30 AM	43 rds. on house in AUCHY. A.29.a 35.60. By order of ADBHY GROUP	WARR
"	"	11.5	Mine exploded 80 yds close to RWF trenches, 15th fired on trench junction just N. of MINE POINT. A.17 B & 7.9	WARR
"	30.5.16	5 PM	Small shrapnel over trenches firing Ute shot on support position.	WARR

Lt. Campbell received a commission into Staff Battn. Sub. in the month to men joined batty. One man killed, three wounded at our batt. which includes S.S. stranged Capt. ..... joined up to # Q 167 Bde.

Lt. Campbell posted to # Q 167 Bde on D/166 Howitzer Battery

Glow Battn. were posted to 166 Bde.

W. Mawkesley RFA Lieut. D 166 Bde RFA

Army Form C. 2118.

833/ June / 166 Bde RFA

Vol 6

WAR DIARY
INTELLIGENCE SUMMARY.
(Erase heading not required.)

Instructions regarding War Diaries and Intelligence Summaries are contained in F. S. Regs., Part II. and the Staff Manual respectively. Title pages will be prepared in manuscript.

Place	Date	Hour	Summary of Events and Information	Remarks and references to Appendices
	JUNE 1916.			
GORRE	10th		Lieut.H.A.Littlejohn posted from 459th Battery R.F.A. to take temporary command of A/166.	
GORRE	17th		Col.A.H.S.Goff (166 Bde.H.Q.) took over command of GIVENCHY Group.	
GORRE	24th		Col.Rochford Boyd (156 Bde.H.Q.) relieved Col.A.H.S.GOFF and took over command of GIVENCHY Group. 166 Bde.H.Q. returned to BETHUNE.	
GORRE	25th		Lieut.E.G.Lutyens Adjutant 166 Bde. posted to command A/156 with effect from 28/5/16, vice Capt.L.Hill to England (sick).	

E C Ormond
2nd Lieut
for A/A Col.

COMMANDING 166TH BRIGADE, R.F.A.

June
D/166 R.F.A.
Vol 1

WAR DIARY
INTELLIGENCE SUMMARY

Army Form C. 2118

Place	Date	Hour	Summary of Events and Information	Remarks and references to Appendices
ANNEQUIN	6 June	6.30 pm	Battery fired on the advance by attached Officers D/305.	4/35
"	7 June 12-1 pm		Registered trench junctions with N.C.T. charges.	4/1
	9 June to 12 June	3 pm	Fired on Craters at MAD POINT + continued at intervals varying from 20 to 40 min until 25 pm 12th June. about 250 rounds.	4/2
	10 June	2 am	Battery fired in support after explosion of enemy mine at A27 to 65.45.	4/3
	13-15 June	-	Foggy quiet days. battery did not fire.	4/4
	16 June	4.30 am	At 11 pm on 15th night there was advanced on fire in stores. Battery fired 10 rds on on Trench Junctions.	4/5
	17 June	1.30 am	Battery retaliated to bombardment of trenches by enemy following raid carried out by Cumerlay Scots at midnight.	4/6
	18 June	6 pm	Registered Trench junction with Aeroplane observation.	4/7
	19 June to 30 June	11 am	During the morning rounds were fired on registered points to test new shell (Mk VI) a Mfg. Emplacement was knocked out.	4/8

WAR DIARY or INTELLIGENCE SUMMARY

Army Form C. 2118

(Erase heading not required.)

Instructions regarding War Diaries and Intelligence Summaries are contained in F.S. Regs., Part II. and the Staff Manual respectively. Title Pages will be prepared in manuscript.

Place	Date	Hour	Summary of Events and Information	Remarks and references to Appendices
ANNEQUIN	23 Jun		During the morning registrations were carried out without ill effect.	
	25 and	2.15 pm	30 rounds were fired on trench junction in A 28 c by batn of CUINCHY Rifle Group - blward.	4/55
	25 Jun		30 "6" shells fell near ANNEQUIN 9 am. Very quiet during remainder of day.	
	26 Jun	12 noon	Enemy fired on a new win. WESTERN PT. We fired 10 rounds A 24 & 95.50.	4/55
			Remainder of the day quiet. During the evening Registration of A 29 c 85.20 was made by Aeroplane observation.	
	24 June	11.15 am	In compliance with program of group 10 rounds were fired on LES BRIQUES A 22 d 4.9, and at 3.10 pm 40 rounds on MAD HIGGAS CAR TRENCH	4/55 4/55
		3.0 pm	The Enemy put up a mine at MINE PT. The battery retaliated by firing on two front line trenches at this point.	
		4.0 pm	Registration by Aeroplane was carried out on trench Junctions A 29 c 47 & A 22 c 9.11	4/35
	25 June	4.0 pm	40 rounds were fired on N of Craters at MAD PT. Battery employed will group scheme	
		10 am	40 rounds were fired on RAILWAY trench	
		5.10 am	Battn (relief) of CUINCHY Sub group fired retaliations. Gun fired on an ANTI AIR CRAFT Sgt at A 20 b 3.4	
		3.40 pm	Enemy put up a mine 6 of MINE PT. Big fires on ————— RAILWAY trench & Ground Jnct A 28 a 20.35.	
		9.40 pm	30 rounds on RAILWAY PT A 28 c 3.2 - in compliance will GROUP scheme.	
	26 Jun	10.30 pm		
		1 pm	Registration on MAD PT Craters & front line trench	4/55
		6.55 pm	Enemy put up mine at MINE PT. Battery retaliated on trench at A 27 b 40.95	
	27 Jun	11.5 pm	40 rounds on craters near MAD POINT - according to program of Group.	4/55
		3.15 am	40 rounds }	
		11.30 pm	The Battery assisted the Infantry in a successful raid on the Enemy Trenches near MAD PT. We fired 120 guns with on MAD POINT CRATERS, then putting a barrage of on the following trench	4/55
	28 Jun	to 12 a.m	Junctions A28c25.45 A 28 d 6.9. A 28 d 90.95 A 22 d ac 15 M 28 b 10.25	
		11.30 pm	A trolling Salvo was fired from MADAGASCAR & RAILWAY TRENCHES	

Army Form C. 2118

WAR DIARY
or
INTELLIGENCE SUMMARY
(Erase heading not required.)

Instructions regarding War Diaries and Intelligence Summaries are contained in F. S. Regs., Part II. and the Staff Manual respectively. Title Pages will be prepared in manuscript.

Place	Date	Hour	Summary of Events and Information	Remarks and references to Appendices
ANNEQUIN	28 Tues (cont)	4.15pm	Enemy exploded a mine N. of MAD PT. The battery retaliated on from that trench immediately	9/11
	29 Wed	11.35am	The Battery was invited by a Russian General & Staff. We fired about a dozen rounds on enemy trenches at MAD PT. for their kinematograph.	9/11
		9.15pm	Twenty rounds on MADAGASCAR trench. Group program	9/11
		10.10 to 11.0 pm	About sixty rounds on trench at A 2 B C 9.4 + retaliation was asked for	
	30 Thur	9.50am	Fired on trench A 2 9 d 6.4	9/11
		11.0	A suspected O.P. was bombarded - result unknown.	
		4.15pm	Thirty rounds were fired on RAILWAY POINT.	

Signed H Flanders Lt for O/C
O/166

1875 Wt. W593/826 1,000,000 4/15 J.B.C. & A. A.D.S.S./Forms/C. 2118.

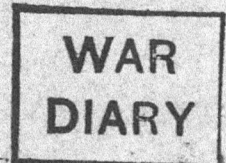

Headquarters,

166th BRIGADE, R.F.A.

(33rd Division)

J U L Y

1 9 1 6

WAR DIARY
INTELLIGENCE SUMMARY

166th Brigade R.F.A. Vol 7

Place	Date	Hour	Summary of Events and Information	Remarks and references to Appendices
ANNEQUIN BETHUNE	6th & night of 7th		Relieved by 39th Division.	
	8th		Brigade marched to & billeted at L'ECLEME	
	9th		Entrained at LILLERS. Detrained at SAULIEUX. marched to & billeted at AROUVES.	
	10th		Left AROUVES. marched to & billeted at CROUY.	
	12th		Left CROUY. marched to & bivouaced at VERQUEMONT.	
	13th		Left VERQUEMONT. marched to & bivouaced at TREUX. 2/Lt S.N. Sloane admitted to hospital sick.	
			2/Lt J.A. Lort joined & posted to B/166. 2/Lt Y.A.D. Kalooln joined & posted to C/166	
			Left TREUX & marched to FRICOURT. 2/Lt C.N. Wakes & Lt C.R.G. Wadman admitted to hospital sick.	
	14th		of 1000 yds line. with shrapnel & lachrymatory. 2/Lt H.H. Hewitt & 2/Lt Y.C. Kerr wounded.	
			Brigade went into action 800x E of MAMETZ WOOD (SOMME)	
	15th		R/L DM Hill killed in action.	
	16th		B/L B.J. Elliott wounded & reported missing. Believed to be prisoner of war.	
	19th		Colonel R.H.S. Goff wounded	
			Major D. Stewart, 167th Brigade R.F.A. assumed temporary command of 166th Brigade R.F.A.	
	20th		2/Lt A. Hirst, X/33. T.M.B. attached to B/166.	
	23rd		Lt J.A. McCallum joined & posted to D/166. 2/Lt H.K. Briggs joined & posted to B/166	
	24th		2/Lt H.K. Briggs killed in action. Capt N.G.J. Buxton wounded in action.	
	25th		Capt. D. Sloane rejoined 166th Brigade R.F.A & assumed 18 command 166th Brigade R.F.A.	
	26th		2/Lt N. Hayter joined & posted to B/166.	
	27th		Major A.D. Murray joined & assumed command of 166th Brigade. Lt. F.H. Beresford joined	
			& posted to A/166, 2/Lt 6.6. Lewis, 2/Lt A.H. Viking Jones & posted to B.C & D Batteries respectively	
	29th		Total Casualties during month :-	

Officers:
Killed... 3
Wounded... 8 (1 accidentally)
1 Wounded & missing.

Other Ranks:
Killed... 7
Wounded... 41
Missing, believed to be prisoners of war... 3

S.M.Murri Lt. Col.
COMMANDING 166TH BRIGADE, R.F.A.

33rd Divisional Artillery

166th BRIGADE

ROYAL FIELD ARTILLERY

AUGUST 1916

Army Form C. 2118.

WAR DIARY
or
INTELLIGENCE SUMMARY.

(Erase heading not required.)

166th Brigade. R.F.A.

No 8

Place	Date	Hour	Summary of Events and Information	Remarks and references to Appendices
August 1916	2nd		Relieved by 17th Divl Arty. & proceeded to DERNANCOURT.	
	4th		2/Lt. A.J. MINSON & 2/Lt. E.C. ORMOND wounded. 2/Lt. T.Q. HARVEY joined & posted to B & D/166 respectively.	
	9th		Capt. A. MAXWELL joined & posted to D/166. 2/Lt. H.O. MOCATTA joined & posted to C/166	
	10th		2/Lt. A. HEADS attached from V/33 T.M. Batty. rejoined his unit.	
	11.		2/Lt. J.A. TAIT transferred from A/166 to Bde. H.Q. to take up duties of Orderly Officer (vice 2/Lt. E.C. ORMOND wounded & invalided to ENGLAND.	
			Brigade left DERNANCOURT & relieved 156th Brigade R.F.A. In action at S.20.a.7.6.d. East of MAMETZ WOOD (SOMME).	
	13th		Capt. A. MAXWELL D/166 admitted to hospital & invalided to ENGLAND on account of old wounds.	
	15.		2/Lt. C.S. PEERLESS C/166 killed in action.	
	16th		2/Lt. N. HAYLETT B/166 wounded.	
	19th		2/Lt. N. HAYLETT B/166 died of wounds.	
	20th		2/Lt. D.G. CARY-ELWES joined & posted to B/166.	
	22nd		2/Lt. H.O. MOCATTA admitted to hospital suffering from gas poisoning.	
	24th		Supported 33rd Division in operation ordered in O.O. 38 (attacked) Brigade zone 650x frontage about 200x N.W. from DELVILLE WOOD + 1300x S.E. from HIGH WOOD.	
	25th		2/Lt. D. FITCH & 2/Lt. N.T.T. ATHERTON joined & posted to B & C/166 respectively.	
	30th		2/Lt. C.H. WEEKES reposted to C/166 from R.H. & R.F.A. Base Depot.	
			Total casualties for month:- Officers:- 1 killed. 1 died of wounds. 1 wounded. 1 invalided to England O.R's:- 5 killed (3 died of wounds) 25 wounded	

SMMurray Lt. Col.
COMMANDING 166TH BRIGADE R.F.A.

SECRET.

Copy No. 6

14th Divisional Artillery Operation Order No.58
By
Brigadier General W.Sandys, C.M.G.

Reference Map 1/10,000 Nos.X.17 and X.18.

1. On August 24th the 14th Divisional Artillery, plus 2 Brigades R.F.A. of 33rd Division will support the 33rd Division in operations ordered in 33rd Division Operation Order No.66 (copy attached).

2. Procedure will be as per Time Table attached. This time table does not refer to 46th and 47th Brigades R.F.A. except as regards their Howitzer batteries, nor to T.M.Batteries.

3. From 3.30 p.m. on August 24th, 46th and 47th Brigades will be responsible for zones as follows :-
    46th Bde for normal zones of 46th and 47th Bdes
    47th Bde for normal zones of 48th and 49th Bdes.

4. From 3.45 p.m. to 7.45 p.m. 18 pounder batteries of 46th and 47th Brigades will bombard the enemy's front line trenches in above zones and areas in rear, with occasional short bursts of rapid fire on the front line from 3.50 p.m. onwards. Rate of fire about 1 round per gun per 2 minutes.
    O.C.,46th Brigade will detail 2 Sections 18 pounders for counter battery work only during the operations.
    A list of hostile batteries will be forwarded on the morning of August 24th of which as many as possible should be engaged.
    Between 4.45 p.m. and 6.50 p.m., 46th and 47th Brigades will keep a proportion of rounds continually on the German Front Line to cover the fire of our Trench Mortars.

5. Trench Mortars.
    Trench Mortars will engage objectives as under :-
    4.45 p.m. to 6.50 p.m. - 14th Division Mediums engage New Trench running from S.11.a.2.3 to S.11.b.0.5½.
    -do- 33rd Division Mediums engage WOOD LANE in S.4.d.and S.10.b.
    -do- V/14 Heavy T.M. engage New Trench running from S.11.a.2.3 through S.11.b.0.5½.
    In all cases as many rounds as possible will be fired.
    O.C.,V/14 will fire one ranging round before 3.45 p.m.

6. In all cases where Brigades are given the same objective, each Brigade will cover the whole of it to ensure that there are no gaps.

7. (a) From 8.45 p.m. onwards, and until further orders, 46th and 47th Brigades will be responsible for the support of zones allotted in para 3.

   (b) For offensive and defensive action zones of remaining Brigades will be as stated in period 7.5 p.m. to 7.45 p.m. of Time Table.

   (c) For S.O.S. purposes all 4.5" Howitzer Batteries will normally open on objectives given in period 6.45 p.m. to 6.50 p.m of Time Table, or other objectives as situation demands.

-2-

8. New O.P's and communications will be established as soon as possible on the New Front.

9. Maps showing barrage lines are attached.
As these lines are inaccurate, these will not be used for allotting tasks. For this purpose the co-ordinates given in this order will be used.

10. No dates or times will be sent by telephone.

11. Reference 33rd Division O.O.56, the ZERO hour to-morrow August 24th will be 5.45 pm

12. Acknowledge.

[signature]

Major R.A.

Brigade Major R.A.

23/8/16. 14th (Light) Division.

Issued at 8 p.m.

```
Copy No. 1 to 46th Bde )
         2    47th Bde ) Copies of Time Table issued
         3    48th Bde )  on scale of 1 per battery
         4    49th Bde )
         5   162nd Bde )
         6   166th Bde )
         7    D.T.M.O.,14th Div.
         8    D.T.M.O.,33rd Div.
         9    O.C.,V/14 H.T.M.
    10 & 11)
    12 & 13)33rd Div.G.S.
    and 14 )
        15    R.A.,XV Corps.
        16    33rd D.A.
        17    7th D.A.
        18    1st D.A.
        19    Staff Captain.
    20 & 21 War Diary.
        22    File.
```

Time Table to accompany 14th Div'l Artillery Operation Order No.38.

Date August 24th.

Time.	Brigade.	Procedure.
5.45 p.m. to 5.15 p.m.	133th Brigade.	18 pounders. 3 Batteries on TEA TRENCH from S.12.a.3¾.5 to S.11.b.5¼.5. also search ground and communication trenches West of FLERS-LONGUEVAL Road inclusive. 1 Round per gun per 2 minutes.
5.15 p.m. to 5.50 p.m.	133th Brigade	18 pounders. 3 Batteries on New Trench from S.12.c.0.7 to S.11.b.6.3. Searching in rear to be continued. 1 Round per gun per 2 minutes.
5.45 p.m. to 5.50 p.m.	48th Brigade	18 Pounders. 3 Batteries on TEA TRENCH from S.12.a.3¾.5 to S.11.b.5¾.5. Also search ground in rear as for 166th Brigade, 1 round per gun per 2 minutes.
5.50 p.m.	D/48th Bde.	Bombard TEA TRENCH, 1 round per gun per minute.
-do-	162nd Brigade	18 Pounders. 3 Batteries bombard New Trench from S.11.b.6.3 to S.11.a.7.5, ground and communication trenches in rear. 1 Round per gun per 2 minutes.
-do-	D/162nd Bde.	TEA TRENCH, TEA LANE and TEA SUPPORT (West of FLERS-LONGUEVAL Road), but chiefly on TEA TRENCH. 1 Round per gun per minute.
-do-	49th Brigade.	18 Pounders. 1 Battery New Trench from S.11.b.6.3 to S.11.a.7.5. 2 Batteries New Trench from S.11.a.7.5 to S.11.a.3.2. Also search ground in rear. 1 Round per gun per 2 minutes
-do-	D/47th Bde. D/49th Bde.	New Trench from S.11.b.6.4 to S.11.a.9.5¼.) 1 Round per gun per minute New Trench from S.11.a.9.5½ to S.11.a.3.2.)
5.45 p.m. to 6.50 p.m.	162nd Bde.	Gun of 162nd Brigade to shell New Trench about 1 round per minute, last ten minutes 2 rounds a minute. To retain at least 150 rounds and be ready in the event of a counter attack.
5.50 p.m. to 6.45 p.m.	A 1 1 D/46,D/47,D/48 and D/162	18 Pounders. Continue as before. 1½ rounds per gun per minute. Continue as before at same rate of fire.

(cont. -2-)

Time.	Brigade.	Procedure.
6.45 p.m. to 6.50 p.m.	All	18 Pounders, continue and open an intense shrapnel fire at 4 rounds per gun per minute. continue and open an intense shrapnel fire at 4 rounds per gun per minute. 4.5" Hows. lift to objectives further back at 1 round per Howitzer per 2 minutes as follows:- D/162 - FLERS-LONGUEVAL Road but not South of S.12.b.0.6½. Special attention to trench junctions. D/48 - TEA LANE and TEA SUPPORT. D/47 - COFFEE LANE and its junction with SWITCH LANE. D/46 - SWITCH TRENCH between S.5.central and S.6.c.2¼.6½. 1 Round per Howitzer per 2 minutes.
6.50 p.m to 7.5 p.m.	All Howitzers All Brigades.	Continue on last objectives at 1 round per Howitzer per 2 minutes. All 13 Pounders search back by 25 yards at a time at 1 minute intervals (no cessation of firing) until they arrive at a line S.12.a.6.4 - S.12.a.0.7. thence to WOOD LANE at S.11.a.0.7. Rate of fire 18prs - 4 rds per gun per min. The 5 - 18 Pounder Batteries of 48th Brigade on TEA TRENCH will not commence lifting until 6.54 p.m. Barrage will lift / or via L.P into next zone except S.11.a.67. Zones for this barrage will be as follows :- 166th Bde - S.12.a.6.4 to S.12.a.0.7. 48th Bde - S.12.a.0.7 to S.11.b.5.7. 162nd Bde - S.11.b.5.7 to S.11.a.6½.7. 48th Bde - S.11.a.6½.7 to S.11.a.0.7. } Sweeping fire in all cases.
7.5 p.m. to 7.45 p.m	All	Alternate Sections 18prs (1, 3, and 5 from Right of Brigades) search ground etc behind, remainder continue close barrage by sweeping. Zones for searching purposes will be taken as being between North and South lines running through points in previous paragraph except the right of 166th Brigade which will extend to FLERS-LONGUEVAL Road inclusive. Afterwards 1 Rate of fire - first 10 minutes - 2 rounds per gun per minute. 1 round per gun per minute.
7.45 to 8.45pm	All	Rates of fire will be halved if situation permits.
8.45 p.m.	All	4.5" Hows fire will become intermittent and will gradually die down, but will not cease before daylight. 18prs cease close barrage but continue to search ground behind and all approaches and trenches within range at frequent intervals, throughout the night. Batteries will be particularly alert for S.O.S.Signal.

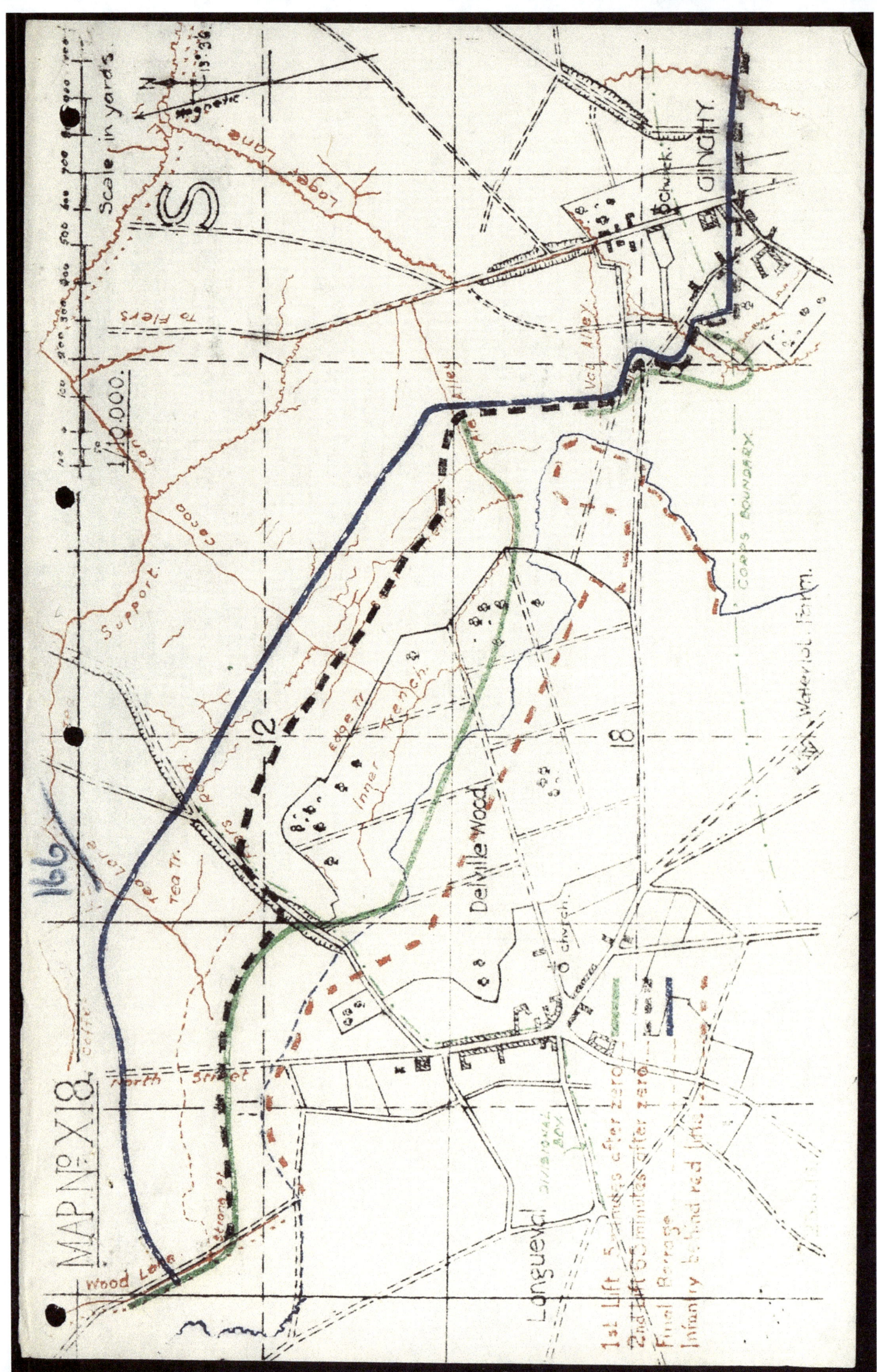

Supported 33a Division in
Operations ordered in O.O. 38 (attached.)
Brigade Zone 650ˣ frontage about 200ˣ NW from Delville
Wood & 1300ˣ SE from Highwood.

33

Army Form C. 2118.

166th Brigade R.F.A.
Vol 4

WAR DIARY
or
INTELLIGENCE SUMMARY.
(Erase heading not required.)

Instructions regarding War Diaries and Intelligence Summaries are contained in F.S. Regs., Part II and the Staff Manual respectively. Title pages will be prepared in manuscript.

September 1916.

Place	Date	Hour	Summary of Events and Information	Remarks and references to Appendices
MAMETZ (SOMME)	1st		2/Lt. G.R.G. Collins admitted to Hospital suffering from gas poisoning.	
"	2nd		Lt. Col. A.D. Murray, 2/Lt. J.A. Tait, & Lieut. F.R. Beresford admitted hospital suffering from gas poisoning. Capt. T.E. Divrie B/166 assumed command of Brigade.	
"	5th		Relieved by 1st N.Z.F.A. Bde. Brigade proceeded to LA NEUVILLE.	
"	6th		Brigade proceeded to FLESSELLES. 12/Lt. J.J. Gorman posted to D/166. 2/Lt. D. Fitch B/166 transferred to 167th Bde.	
"	7th		" " OUTREBOIS.	
"	8th		" " LUCHEUX.	
"	9th			
"	10th		" " MONTENESCOURT.	
"	12th		Batteries relieved Batteries of 126th Brigade.	
	13th		C/166 absorbed. Brigade consists of 26-gun 18-pr Batteries & 1 4.5" gun How Batty. Lt. Col. (C. Stewart Chpt., D.S.O.) assumed command of Brigade. Lieut. J. Campbell joined from 167th Bde. & took over duties of Orderly Officer. 166 Brigade H.Q. took over command of H. Group. - relieving 126 Brigade R.F.A. 37th Div. Relieved by 63rd Bde R.F.A. 12th Div. & proceeded to COUTURETTE. 2/Lt N.H. Milner admitted to hospital suffering from dysentery. Capt. The Hon. T.P.P. Butler attached to B/166.	
	15th			
	16th		Brigade proceeded to GOMMECOURT. Wagon line at GUADIEMPRE.	
ARRAS	17th		Relieved 17th Div. Arty. at SAILLY-AU-BOIS.	
	20th		Relieved by 46th Div. Arty. Brigade proceeded to SOMERIN.	
	22nd		Brigade proceeded to MONTENESCOURT.	
	23rd		Relieved 63rd Bde. & took over command of H. Group. at ARRAS.	
	24th		Capt. T.E. Divrie admitted to hospital. Capt. the Hon. T.P.P. Butler assumed command of B/166	
	30			

Stewart
Lt Col
COMMANDING 166TH BRIGADE.R.F.A.

Army Form C. 2118.

WAR DIARY
or
INTELLIGENCE SUMMARY.

(Erase heading not required.)

166 Brigade. R.F.A. Vol 10

October 1916

Instructions regarding War Diaries and Intelligence Summaries are contained in F.S. Regs., Part II. and the Staff Manual respectively. Title pages will be prepared in manuscript.

Place	Date	Hour	Summary of Events and Information	Remarks and references to Appendices
ARRAS	1st		2/Lr. H.H. Hewitt reported to A/166	
	3rd		Brigade withdrew from ARRAS & proceeded to wagon lines at MONTENESCOURT	
	4th		Wagon Lines moved to GUADIEMPRÉ.	
	5th		Batteries & Bde. H.Q. went into action North of FONQUEVILLERS	
	10th		Batteries shifted into action North of HEBUTERNE. Brigade. H.Q. at SAILLY-AU-BOIS	
			Wagon lines at COUIN.	
	27th		Captain. N.C. Deeming B/166 returned from Hospital.	
			Major R.H.D. Thompson joined & posted to B/166	
	9,2nd		Capt. the Hon. T.P.T. Butler ceased to be attached to B/166.	

Sm Nova
Lt Adjutant. 166 Brigade R.F.A.

SECRET.   33rd D.A., B.M./S/961.

   156th Brigade, R.F.A.
   162nd Brigade, R.F.A.
   166th Brigade, R.F.A.
   R.A. XII Corps.   )
   31st Division.   ) For information.
   92nd Infantry Brigade.   )
   3rd Divisional Artillery.)

1. With reference to the operations to be carried out on "Z" day :-

   The following extracts from 31st Division Order No. 75 and 92nd Infantry Brigade Order No. 73 are forwarded for your information :-

   EXTRACTS FROM 31st Division Order No. 75 dated 3.11.16.

   "1. In continuation of Operation Order No. 70, additional "operations will be undertaken by the 92nd Infantry Brigade "to capture the German Trenches leading from K.23.b.60 and "K.23.b.93 to THE POINT - K.23.b.18.

   "2. These operations will only be undertaken after the German "lines between K.23.b.60 and K.23.d.96 and between K.23.b.93 "and K.24.c.15 have been taken, and only if the G.O.C. 92nd "Infantry Brigade, or an officer on the spot deputed by him "is of opinion that the task can be undertaken with the force "at his disposal, and at least 1 tank is available as detailed.

   "3. At Zero ∔ 2 hours, 30 minutes, the tanks co-operating with "the Division will arrive at points K.23.b.60 and K.23.b.93 "and will proceed to move close along the trenches leading to "THE POINT.   above

   "4. The 92nd Infantry Brigade will detail a force with advanced "bombing parties to follow the tanks down these trenches, to "clear them up, and to consolidate them. Strong points will "be made near K.23.b.37 and between that place and K.23.b.93. "The 92nd Inf. Bde. will detail a fresh force to take over this "line after dusk on "Z" night, and to carry on with its "consolidation."

   EXTRACTS FROM Additions and Amendments to 92nd Inf. Bde. Order No. 73 dated 2.11.16.

   "(1) Should attack be successful and the enemy found demoral- "ised, and not holding his first and second line strongly from "Point 60 to THE POINT and from Point 93 to THE POINT, these "two lines will be captured and consolidated.
   "In the event of this secondary operation taking place, "BLIND "ALLEY" will be opened up as a communication trench by parties "of the 12th K.O.Y.L.I. when the enemy's barrage slackens or at "dusk, and the front line consolidated by night across "No Man's "Land" to join up with THE POINT, under arrangements to be made "by 94th Brigade. The 94th Brigade will find the garrison for "this trench.
   "The above secondary operation will not commence (on account of "protective barrage) until Zero ∔ 2½ hours.
   "The O.C. E.Y.R. will decide whether the operation will take "place or not".

2. The above additional operation has necessitated the extension of the Blue line A ----- A on map previously sent you Northwards along WALTER trench to its junction with SNUFF ALLEY for final

barrage - See XIII Corps Artillery Instructions No. 15 para. 9 (c) This extension of Barrage will be found by 166th Brigade, R.F.A. on completing their trench barrage and reaching the Red line.

3. The following addition should therefore be made to Trench Barrage:-
At Zero + 0.30 minutes.

166th Brigade, R.F.A. leave the Red line B ---- B on map and extend the barrage Blue line A ---- A Northwards along WALTER trench to its junction with SNUFF ALLEY (K.23.b.96.95).

4. Barrage Table for trench barrage issued with 33rd Divisional Artillery Order No. 63 should therefore be added to accordingly.

5. XIII Corps Artillery Instructions No. 11 are cancelled and XIII Corps Artillery Instructions No. 15 are substituted for them for compliance. Copy herewith.

6. The above paragraphs are to be read in conjunction with and in addition to 33rd D.A. Operation Order No. 63 which holds good (less paras. 2 & 6) which are cancelled.

7. LIAISON OFFICERS. These will now be

H.Q. 31st Division Captain E.G. Lutyens, R.F.A.
H.Q. 92nd Inf. Bde. Major J.D. Belgrave, D.S.O., R.F.A.
Hdqrs. Right Battalion furnished by 156th Brigade, R.F.A.
" Left Battalion furnished by 162nd Brigade, R.F.A.

8. PERMANENT BARRAGE POINTS FOR 4.5" Hows.

Trench Junctions at
D/166th Bde. R.F.A. .... L.19.c.2.5 and L.19.c.05.55
D/156th " L.19.c.4.3
D/162nd " .... L.19.d.15.15.

9. Acknowledge.

H.K.Sadler.

Major, R.A.,
11.11.16. Brigade Major 33rd Divisional Artillery.
Issued at 2 p.m.

TABLE "A"   A.166.

TIME	OBJECTIVE	RATE	PROJ:	REMARKS.
Zero to +0.06	German Support line K.23.d.8.0. to K.24.c.10.75.	3. R.P.G.	A.	
+0.06 to +0.09	Guns shooting S. of SERHEB Rd.only German 3rd line K.30.a.1.9. to K.24.c.62.45. Remainder as before.	Ditto	A.	Guns shooting S. of SERHEB RD. lift at +0.06.
+0.09 to +0.18	All guns. German 3rd line K.30.a.1.9 to K.24.c.70.70.	Ditto	A.	Guns N. of SERHEB RD lift at +0.09.
+0.18 to +0.30	Barrage line. K.24.d.25.20. – K.24.d.10.70. – K.24.a.63.05.	2. R.P.G	50% A 50% AX.	All guns lift at +0.18.
+0.30 till further orders	All guns barrage line K.24.a.10.78 to K.23.b.96.95	3 R.P.G per 2 min	50% A. 50% AX	All guns switch at +0.30.

TABLE A   A.166.

TIME	OBJECTIVE	RATE	PROJ:	REMARKS.
Zero to +0.06	German Support line K.23.d.8.0. to K.24.c.10.75	3.R.P.G.	A.	
+0.06 to +0.09	Guns Shooting S. of SERHEB Rd. only Guns on 3rd line K.30.a.1.9. to K.24.c.12.05. Remainder as before.	Ditto	A.	Guns shooting S. of SERHEB RD. lift at +0.06.
+0.09 to +0.18	All guns. Guns on 3rd line K.30.a.1.9 to K.24.c.70.70.	Ditto	A.	Guns N. of SERHEB RD lift at +0.09.
+0.18 to +0.30	Barrage line K.24.d.35.20 – K.24.d.10.70. – K.24.a.63.05	2.R.P.G	50% A. 50% AX.	All guns lift at +0.18.
+0.30 till further orders.	All guns barrage line K.24.a.10.70 to K.23.b.96.95	3.R.P.G. per 2 min	50% A. 50% AX.	All guns switch at +0.30.

TABLE A   B.166.

TIME	OBJECTIVE	RATE	PROJ	REMARKS
Zero to +0.09	[illegible] K.24.c.10.75 – K.23.[?].50	R.G.	A.	
+0.09 to +0.18	[illegible] K.24.c.10.70 – K.24.a.15.56	Ditto	A	Rate goes – 1½/gun to +0.09
+0.18 to +0.30	[illegible] K.24.a.6.0 [illegible] K.24.a.3.50	½ R.G.	[illegible]	[illegible] K.24.a.13.05 [illegible] K.24.a.b2.05 K.24.a.10.70
+0.30 [illegible]	[illegible]	R.G.	50% H.E. 50% [illegible]	All guns cease at +0.30

TABLE 'A'   B. 166.

TIME.	OBJECTIVE	RATE	PROJ.	REMARKS.
Zero to +0.09	German Support line K.24.c.10.75 - K.23.b.80.50	3 R.P.G.	A.	
+0.09 to +0.18	German 2nd line trench K.24.c.70.70 - K.24.a.15.75	Ditto	A	All guns lift at +0.09
+0.18 to +0.30	Guns S. of K.24.a.63.05. Barrage line from K.24.b.05.05 to K.24.d.10.70. Remainder as before.	2 R.P.G.	50% A. 50% Ax.	Guns S. of K.24.a.63.05. lift in battery zone to line K.24.a.63.05 - K.24.d.10.70
+0.30 till further orders.	Barrage line, German 3rd line trench from K.24.a.10.78 (incl) to K.24.a.40.70 (incl) (HALTER STREET)	3 R.P.G. per 2 mins	50% A. 50% Ax.	All guns switch at +0.30.

TABLE 6						D.166

TIME	OBJECTIVE	RATE	PROJ	REMARKS
Zero to +0.09	German support trench Point a.1.0 to R.22.7.8	R.P.G.	Bx.	
+0.09 to +0.18	German front line trench from R.22.a.6.5 to R.22.a.15.75	Lift	Bx.	all guns lift as +0.09
+0.18 to +1 hour	Ditto	Lift	Bx.	lift at +0.18
+1 hour on	Prominent barrage points. Roads at road junction at R.22.a.5.5 Cross roads R.a.a R.22.a.5.5	½ R.P.G. per min.	Bx	

TABLE 'A'   D.166.

TIME.	OBJECTIVE.	RATE.	PROJ.	REMARKS.
Zero to +0.09	German Support line K.24.a.1.0. to K.23.b.8.5.	2 RPG per min.	B x.	
+0.09 to 0.18	German 3rd line trench from K.24.a.6.2. to rd. at K.24.a.15.75.	Ditto	B x.	All guns left as +0.09
+0.18 to +1 hour	Ditto	1 RPG per min	B x.	No lift at +0.18
+1.00 hour til further orders.	Permanent barrage points 2 guns on tr. rd. junction at L.19.c.2.5. 2 guns trench junction at L.19.c.05.5.	½ RPG Diff per min.	B x.	

WAR DIARY
or
INTELLIGENCE SUMMARY.

Army Form C. 2118.

NOVEMBER 1916

166th Brigade R.F.A.

Vol XI

Place	Date	Hour	Summary of Events and Information	Remarks and references to Appendices
	1st		2/Lt. H.D. Malcolm transferred from A to D/166	
	6th		Lt. H.H. Stanford joined & posted to B/166	
	6/7	1. A.M.	Assisted in a raid carried out by 13th & 14th Bns. Yorks & Lancs. Regt. at 1:- am (Copy of orders attached).	
	13th		Took part in the General attack, being the extreme left flank covering the 31st Division Infantry. (Copy of orders attached). Infantry gained first objective & held it, but were forced to retire later owing to lack of support on their flank. Barrage, & wire cut to everyone's satisfaction. Copy of Battalion Commander's letter attached. Enemy retaliation slight.	
	13th		Major R.D.D. Thompson invalided to England.	
	14th		Capt. W.A.H. Barritt & 2/Lt. T.Q. Harvey rejoined & posted to B/166. Capt. Y.H. Dust joined & posted to B/166. 2/Lt. L.W. Porterfield invalided to England.	
	17th		Batteries withdrew to wagon lines at ST LEGER & COUIN.	
	18th		Brigade H.Q. withdrew to wagon line at COUIN.	
	19th		Lt. L.N. Blomenack transferred from B to A/166	
	22nd		Brigade left wagon line & marched to TALMAS.	
	23rd		Brigade left TALMAS & marched to AIRAINES.	

SMMorris Lt.Col.
COMMANDING 166TH BRIGADE R.F.A.

Army Form C. 2118.

WAR DIARY
or
INTELLIGENCE SUMMARY.
(Erase heading not required.)

166th Brigade RFA

Vol 12

Place	Date	Hour	Summary of Events and Information	Remarks and references to Appendices
AIRAINES	1st		Lt. J. Campbell Bde. I.O. admitted to hospital.	
	12th		2/Lt. H.A.D. Malcolm posted from D/166 to X/33 T.M. By.	
	13th		2/Lt. L.M. Blomenstok from A/166 to B/166 T.B.	
	14th		Capt. H. Freeman transferred from B/166 to 33rd D.A.C.	
	28th		Capt. J.R. McCallum transferred from D/166 to B/166	
	28/29		Brigade left AIRAINES + marched to ST SAUVEUR	
	29/30		Brigade marched from St Sauveur to SAILLY-LE-SEC.	
	30/31		Brigade marched from SAILLY-LE-SEC to Camp No. 14.	
	31st		Relieved 156th Brigade R.F.A. in action N. of MAUREPAS.	

Simmons Lt Col.
Commanding 166th Brigade R.F.A.

Army Form C. 2118.

WAR DIARY
or
INTELLIGENCE SUMMARY
(Erase heading not required.)

Ad Qrs. 166 Bde R.F.A.

Vol 14

Place	Date	Hour	Summary of Events and Information	Remarks and references to Appendices
FIELD	12th – 28th	3rd 6/15	166 Bde R.F.A. billeted at BELLOY S. SOMME.	

Arthur Stray.
Lt OC 166 Bde
R.F.A.

Received from Headquarters 33rd Division the under-
mentioned War Diary for Jan. 1917.

----

166 F.A. Bde.   January.

SECRET

33 Div.
G.S.133

D. A. G.,
  G. H. Q.
    3rd Echelon.

   Herewith War Diary for January 1917 of the
166 F.A. Bde.

   Please acknowledge receipt on enclosed slip.

                              B.L. Montgomery Capt
                           for Brigadier General,
9/2/17.   Commanding 33rd Division.

Vol 3
Army Form C. 2118.
166th Bde R.F.A.

WAR DIARY
or
INTELLIGENCE SUMMARY
(Erase heading not required.)

Instructions regarding War Diaries and Intelligence Summaries are contained in F.S. Regs., Part II. and the Staff Manual respectively. Title pages will be prepared in manuscript.

Hour, Date, Place	Summary of Events and Information	Remarks and references to Appendices
Jan 1st 1917	Relieved 156 Bde R.F.A. at BOOM RAVINE. Reorganisation of 33rd Divisional Artillery.	Appendix (1)
14th		
14/31	Bde. H.Q. 166 Bde. billeted at BELLOY-S-SOMME.	

Lothian Nicol
Lt Col
for OC 166 Bde RFA

C O P Y.   Right Battalion.

To/ 92 Infantry Brigade.

   I have talked to most of my remaining N.C.Os. and they all
agree that there was to all intents and purposes no wire that
was in any way an obstacle to the attacking troops. The wire could
not possibly have been better destroyed. All also agree that the
barrage was excellent and that if it had not been for the mud and
for the attacking troops would not have suffered to any appreciable
extent. All ranks hope that the G.O.C. 92 Bde. will be kind
enough to convey their most cordial appreciation of the work of
the R.A.

16.11.16.   (Sd.) K.W.Savery Lt.Col.
                                  Comdg. 13 E. York R.

To/ 92 Infantry Brigade.   Left Battalion.

   The wire in front of the German wire was cut exceedingly
well aaa No wire was standing it was all blown up and lying in
heaps aaa All say that they had no difficulty in getting through
the wire which presented no obstacle aaa The barrage was excellent
aaa Some of my waves followed it very close and reached the
German lines without a single casualty.

16.11.16.   (Sd.) E.J.Wellesley Lt.Col.

                              H.Q. 92nd Infantry Bde.
                                  17th Nov. 1916.

Dear Wade,

   I enclose reports on wire and barrage from my two
Battalion Commanders as I think your Brigade Commanders may like
to see them.

   We are very gratified to you for the great trouble taken
over the wire and realize that our success in getting into the
German lines was due to 33rd Divisional Artillery.

        (Sd.)   H. W. Williams.

D R A F T.   Copy No.

166th Brigade R.F.A., Order No.4.

Ref:- 1/10,000 MARTINSART Map Edition 3 a. dev. 11th. 1916.

1. One copy of D.A., R.M/S/301 d/- 11.11.16. is forwarded herewith
for information; orders to be read in conjunction with 53rd
D.A. Order No.63 d/- 24.10.16.

2. 166th Brigade R.F.A., will take part in the trench barrage
as shown in tables "A" attached.

3. Barrage on enemy's support trench will extend from trench
junction at K.24 c.8.0. to the TOUVENT FARM – LA LOUVIERE
FARM ROAD at K.23 b.80.50 and is allotted to 18-pr Batteries
as below:-

   A/166 from K.23 d.80.00 to K.24 c.10.75 (incl.)

   B/166   ,, K.24 c.10.75 (excl.) to read at K.23 b.86.50.(incl.)
   18-prs will be distributed over battery fronts and will
   sweep.

   C/166 from K.24 a.10.00 to read at K.23 b.85.50.

4. Barrage on enemy 3rd line will extend from K.30. a.10.90 to
the TOUVENT FARM – LA LOUVIERE FARM ROAD at K.24 a.15.75 up
to zero +td 0.30 minutes only.

This is allotted to Batteries as under:-

   A/166 K.30 a.10.90 to K.24 c.70.70 (incl.)

   B/166 K.24 c.70.70 (excl.) to read at K.24 a.15.75 (incl)

   K.24 c.70.70 is where the 120 metre compass crosses the
   German 3rd line trench as new edition 3a MARTINSART Map.

   D/166 from K.24 a.60.20 (incl) to read at K.24 a.15.75 (incl

5. INTERMEDIATE BARRAGE.   A/166 cnl + flank guns B/66.

   At zero + 0.18 will lift from German 3rd line between
                              a.63.00.
   K.30 a.1.9. – K.24 c.70.70 to the line K.24 d.25.20 –
                                                    a.63.05
   K.24 d.10.70 – K.24 c.70.70 and remain on it till + 0.30.

6. At zero + 0.30 minutes A/166 and B/166 will extend the
trench barrage northward from along SALVE TRENCH to its
junction with STUMP ALLEY.

Zones for batteries from + 0.30 minutes will be:-

   A/166 K.23 b.96.90 (incl.) to K.24 a.10.75 (incl.)
   B/166 K.24 a.10.78 (excl.) to K.24 a.40.70.

166th Brigade R.F.A. Order No.4. (Contd.)   Sheet 2.

7. PERMANENT BARRAGES.

For 18-pr batteries these will be from + 0.00 onwards as detailed in para 6.

  B/166 Trench Junction at L.19 c.20.80
           L.19 c.05.50

  from + 1.00 hour onwards.

8. SOUTHERN SAFETY LINE.

The Southern Safety line referred to in D.A. Order (to be issued later) runs from K.24 c.00.20 to K.24 d.50.20, thence to L.29 a.50.00.

9. Acknowledge.

Copy No.1 - A/166.
   2 - B/166.
   3 - D/166.
   4)
   5) - File.
   6)
Table "A" attached.

APPENDIX No 1.

156th Brigade R.F.A.

Headquarters.	Becomes Headquarters 166th Bde and awaits further orders.
"A" Battery.	Nil.
"B" Battery	Nil.
"C" Battery	Nil.
"D" Battery	Receives one Section from D/166th Bde.R.F.A.

166th Brigade R.F.A.

Headquarters.	Becomes Headquarters 156th Bde R.F.A.
"A" Battery	Transferred to 26th Bde R.F.A. lll Corps becomes A/26 Bde.
"B" Battery	Transferred to 93rd Bde R.F.A. xXlV Corps becomes C/93 Bde.
"D" Battery	Right Section complete to 156th BDE R.F.A. Left Section complete to 162nd Bde R.F.A.

www.ingramcontent.com/pod-product-compliance
Lightning Source LLC
Chambersburg PA
CBHW081244170426
43191CB00034B/2031